Let's Read About Insects

ANTS

by Susan Ashley

Reading consultant: Susan Nations, M.Ed., author/literacy coach/consultant

WEEKLY WR READER®
EARLY LEARNING LIBRARY

Please visit our web site at: **www.earlyliteracy.cc**
For a free color catalog describing Weekly Reader® Early Learning Library's
list of high-quality books, call 1-877-445-5824 (USA) or 1-800-387-3178 (Canada).
Weekly Reader® Early Learning Library's fax: (414) 336-0164.

Library of Congress Cataloging-in-Publication Data available upon request from publisher.
Fax (414) 336-0157 for the attention of the Publishing Records Department.

ISBN 0-8368-4050-X (lib. bdg.)
ISBN 0-8368-4057-7 (softcover)

This edition first published in 2004 by
Weekly Reader® Early Learning Library
330 West Olive Street, Suite 100
Milwaukee, WI 53212 USA

Editor: JoAnn Early Macken
Picture research: Diane Laska-Swanke
Art direction and page layout: Tammy Gruenewald

Picture credits: Cover © Kjell Sandved/Visuals Unlimited; title, p. 13 © Scott Camazine;
pp. 5, 7, 15, 21 © Robert & Linda Mitchell; p. 9 © George Loun/Visuals Unlimited;
p. 11 Tammy Gruenewald/© Weekly Reader Early Learning Library, 2004; pp. 17, 19
© James P. Rowan

Printed in the United States of America

1 2 3 4 5 6 7 8 9 08 07 06 05 04

Note to Educators and Parents

Reading is such an exciting adventure for young children! They are beginning to integrate their oral language skills with written language. To encourage children along the path to early literacy, books must be colorful, engaging, and interesting; they should invite the young reader to explore both the print and the pictures.

Let's Read About Insects is a new series designed to help children read about insect characteristics, life cycles, and communities. In each book, young readers will learn interesting facts about the featured insects and how they live.

Each book is specially designed to support the young reader in the reading process. The familiar topics are appealing to young children and invite them to read — and reread — again and again. The full-color photographs and enhanced text further support the student during the reading process.

In addition to serving as wonderful picture books in schools, libraries, homes, and other places where children learn to love reading, these books are specifically intended to be read within an instructional guided reading group. This small group setting allows beginning readers to work with a fluent adult model as they make meaning from the text. After children develop fluency with the text and content, the book can be read independently. Children and adults alike will find these books supportive, engaging, and fun!

— Susan Nations, M.Ed., author, literacy coach, and consultant in literacy development

Ants are social insects. They live in communities, just like people do. An ant community is called a **colony**. The ants in a colony live and work together.

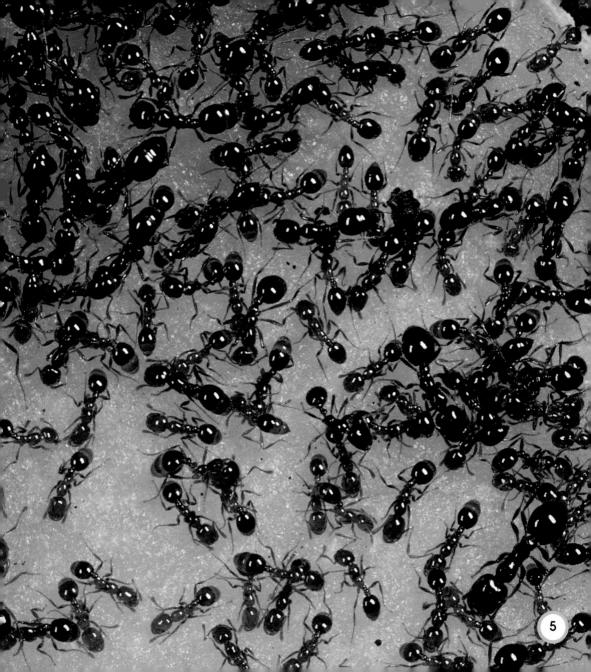

Male ants, a queen ant, and workers live in a colony. Male ants mate with the queen and soon die. The queen spends all her time laying eggs.

queen

Most of the ants in
a colony are workers.
Workers are female
ants. They gather food.
They guard the colony
from enemies. They
work together to raise
the young.

Workers build the colony's home. The home is called a **nest**. Workers dig in the soil with their legs. They carve out hundreds of rooms. Tunnels connect the rooms.

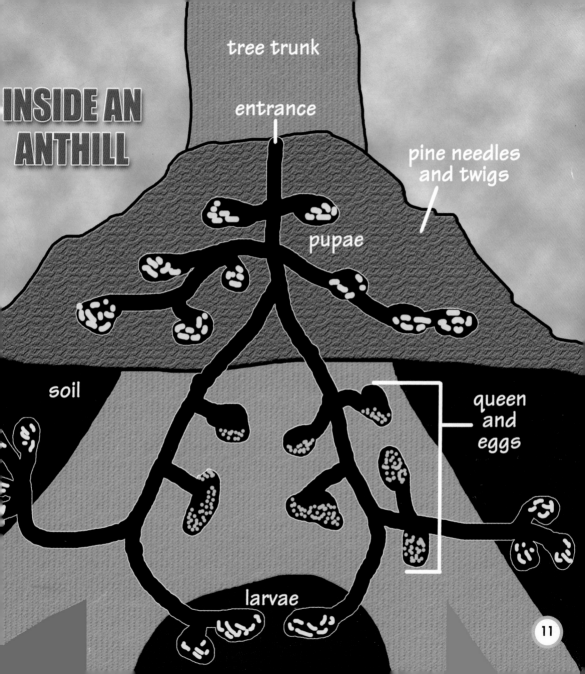

INSIDE AN
ANTHILL

tree trunk

entrance

pine needles
and twigs

pupae

soil

queen
and
eggs

larvae

The queen lays her eggs in one of the rooms. Wormlike larvae hatch from the eggs. Workers clean and feed the larvae in special rooms.

After a few weeks,
the larvae stop eating.
They turn into pupae.
Some types of pupae
wrap up in silk cocoons.
Soon the pupae turn
into fully grown ants.

pupae

larvae

Like all insects, ants have six legs. Ants have two claws on the end of each leg. With their claws, ants can climb up walls. They can even walk upside down!

The two antennae on an ant's head always keep moving. Ants use their antennae to taste, touch, and smell. Ants use their antennae to find food.

Ants may be small, but they are very strong. An ant can lift an object that is twenty times its own weight!

Glossary

antennae — feelers on the head of an insect or animal

cocoons — silk coverings some insects spin to protect themselves in the pupa stage

larvae — the wormlike second stage of growth of some insects

pupae — the third stage of growth of some insects

social — living with others in organized communities

For More Information

Books

Dorros, Arthur. *Ant Cities*. New York: HarperCollins, 1998.

Fowler, Allan. *Inside an Ant Colony*. Danbury, Conn.: Children's Press, 1998.

Hartley, Karen. *Ant*. Chicago: Heinemann Library, 2001.

Vaughan, Jenny. *Ants*. Milwaukee: Gareth Stevens, 1997.

Web Sites

Enchanted Learning

www.ZoomSchool.com/subjects/ insects/ant/

Ant facts and printouts

Index

About the Author

Susan Ashley has written over eighteen books for children, including two picture books about dogs, *Puppy Love* and *When I'm Happy, I Smile*. She enjoys animals and writing about them. Susan lives in Wisconsin with her husband and two frisky felines.